Solving Cold Cases

True Crime Stories that Took Years to Crack

Andrew J. Clark

Disclaimer

Contents

Introduction...1

Chandra Levy 3

  Background Information 3

  The Disappearance 4

  The Investigation...5

  Solving the Case 8

  The Trial 12

  Current Status..18

Robert Peterson, Anton Schuessler, and John Schuessler...19

  Background Information 19

  Discovering the Bodies 21

  The Investigation...22

  The Prime Suspect..24

  The Conviction..25

Lucy Johnson...27

  Background Information 27

  The Disappearance 27

  The Investigation Closing the Case.....................28

  The Reunion 29

Minnie and Ed Maurin 33

  Background Information 33

  The Disappearance 34

  The Investigation...35

The Trial 36

The Verdict 37

Helen Sullivan *39*

Background Information 39

The Crime 39

The Investigation and Fruitless Conclusion 40

Colette Aram..*43*

Background Information 43

The Crime 43

The Investigation 44

Closing the Case 45

A Twist of Fate 47

The Aftermath 47

Linda Strait *49*

Background Information 49

The Disappearance 49

The Investigation 50

A Killer with a Trail of Bodies 51

Closing the Case 52

The Trial 53

Joan Harrison..*55*

Background Information 55

The Crime 55

The Investigation 56

Closing the Case 58

A Twist of Fate 58

Susan Schwarz *61*

Background Information 61

The Crime 61

Voices from Behind the Bars............................62

The Investigation 63

Closing the Case 64

Numerous victims of the BTK killer............................*67*

Background Information 67

The Making of a Criminal 67

A Life of Crime 69

16th Street Baptist Church...*77*

Background Information 77

The Day of the Tragedy 78

The Investigation 80

The Trial 81

Continuing the Investigation and the Trial......................82

The Aftermath 84

Conclusion...*85*

Bonus Chapter from Andrew J. Clark's book Vanished Chilling True Stories of Missing Persons 87

Further Reading...*93*

Introduction

Criminal investigations are often not open-and-shut cases. When we think about crime dramas on the television and the movies, we take for granted the simple procedure they usually display of catching the bad guy; the process by which the investigators get the suspect by piecing together a series of clues. In real life, however, this approach is very rarely as easy. While there may be cases in which the investigators are able to track down a suspect effortlessly, these examples pale in comparison to those cases that demand so much more of officers' time. These can often drag out for weeks, months, or years. In some circumstances, there is simply not enough evidence to track down the perpetrator. The case can seem impossible to solve. When this happens, we are left with what is commonly referred to as a "cold case."

There are many reasons why a case might go cold. A lack of evidence at the scene of the crime is often a major issue. The death of people involved in the event can also lead to difficulties. Something as simple as a detective overlooking one element of the investigation can hinder the entire process. Sometimes, the technology at the disposal of those investigating the crime is simply not advanced enough to solve the case. As these crimes go unsolved and their records are added to the growing mountain of crimes without convictions, it is usually assumed that the case will remain unsolved for the rest of time. However, this is not always true.

Sometimes, the police are able to crack the cold cases. Sometimes, the hard work of those involved can lead to a conviction long after everyone had written off the case as being unsolvable. It might be a criminal finally caving in to their guilt and confessing. It could be a witness's plea bargain. It could be something as simple as a tax error that brings down the whole house of cards. It can even be advances in technology, such as DNA profiling, that allows investigations to make links and deductions that were previously unobtainable. Often, the stories of the cold cases themselves can be just as interesting as the crimes.

In this book, we will search through the long history of criminal investigations and discover some of the most important and fascinating cold cases from around the world. These crimes have been solved through a variety of means, with the detectives involved often battling against years of misfortune and bad luck to finally come face-to-face with the criminal. Read on and discover just what it takes to crack even the coldest of cases.

Chandra Levy

Where: Washington D.C.
When: May 2001
Suspect: Ingmar Guandique
Conviction: November 2010

Background Information

Our first case is a classic example of a complex and unconventional case that became increasingly difficult to solve. The disappearance of Chandra Levy failed to match up with any of the expectations that we might have from watching television and films. Her involvement in the world of politics led many to have conspiratorial views of her eventual demise. The case took nine years to reach a satisfying conclusion. Who exactly was Chandra Levy?

Born on the 14th of April in 1977, Chandra was the daughter of Robert and Susan Levy. They lived in the town of Modesto in California. The family was Jewish and attended a synagogue called Congregation Beth Shalom. Once she had completed high school, Chandra enrolled in San Francisco State University, where she studied for a degree in journalism. From there she took on several intern roles in California while studying for a master's degree focused on public administration.

During the final year of this program, Chandra was required to move to Washington D.C. for another paid intern job. She would be working with the Federal Bureau of Prisons, starting in October of 2000. She worked at the bureau's main offices and was asked to focus chiefly on the public affairs department. Her work was enough to impress her division head, a man named Dan Dunne, who made a special statement on her highly competent approach to dealing with the inquiries from the media pertaining to the upcoming execution of the Oklahoma Bomber, Timothy McVeigh.

At this point, Chandra began to make plans to move in with her boyfriend. She told her landlord, suggesting to him that she was considering breaking her lease to do so. It seems she changed her mind, however, later suggesting to him that the relationship "didn't work out." Despite her good work, Chandra's internship position was terminated in April 2001, as her academic eligibility had expired four months earlier. Having already completed the requirements for her master's degree, Chandra was set to move back to California the following May to attend her graduation.

The Disappearance

The last time anyone saw Chandra Levy alive was on the 1st of May. The DC Metropolitan Police Department was alerted five days later by Chandra's parents, calling from California to say that they had not heard from their child since the beginning of the month. The police department checked the hospitals and Chandra's apartment. Finding no signs of foul play, they reported that to her parents.

The Investigation

Two days later, Chandra's father called the police again to inform them of an affair that had been taking place between his daughter and a Congressman, one he would later say was Gary Condit. The police received corroborating evidence from Chandra's aunt, who had also been told about the relationship. With this information, the local police obtained a search warrant and moved in on Chandra's apartment. During their formal search of the premises, they discovered her identification, her credit cards, and her mobile phone, all stored inside her purse alongside two suitcases that had been partially packed. Her answering machine was full with messages, both from the police and from her family. One police officer attempted to perform a search of the laptop computer inside the apartment, but without the correct training, instead only managed to corrupt the search files.

This information on the laptop would take months for the qualified technicians to reconstruct. After careful analysis and a lot of work, it was discovered that the machine had been used to scour the internet for information regarding "Amtrak," "Baskin-Robbins", "Condit," "Southwest Airlines", and a weather forecast by The Washington Post. The final search on the computer was made to find out more information about the Pierce-Klingle Mansion, the administrative hub of Rock

Creek Park. Police searched the area around the building and nearby roads but found nothing. The investigation was becoming increasingly difficult.

One of the most important threads appeared to be the relationship Chandra shared with Gary Condit, the US Congressman. It didn't take long for the relationship to hit the media. Coupled with Chandra's family holding numerous events and vigils designed to help find their daughter, the news networks had a great deal of material at their disposal. The mantra "bring Chandra home" echoed through all of the family's actions. But for the congressman, more immediate questions were being posed. Condit, a married man, at first denied any involvement with Chandra. Despite the police reiterating that Condit was not a suspect in the case, it was the belief of the family that the Congressman was being purposefully evasive and potentially hiding a clue relating to Chandra's disappearance.

Sources inside the police department who wished to remain anonymous suggested to the media that Condit has confessed to being involved in an extra-marital relationship with Chandra. His descriptions to interviewing officers included his beliefs that she was both a non-smoker and a vegetarian, and that she was due to return to Washington following her graduation. It was a surprise to Condit to learn that Chandra's apartment lease had expired. Police searched the Congressman's home and the home of a flight attendant named Anne Marie Smith. The pair had also been involved in an affair, though Smith had never met Chandra.

Officials began to investigate Condit for a possible obstruction of justice in the case of the missing girl. Noting his annoyance at the media leaks involving his name, Condit refused to participate in a lie detector test with the police department. Instead, his lawyer indicated that he had taken part in a private test and had passed. During a television interview, the Congressman avoided direct questions put to him by the news anchor. The coverage continued to intensify, the pressure rising until the sudden events on the 11th of September, 2001 took over on the front page news. The coverage of Chandra Levy's case diminished, replaced by the geopolitical terrorist attack on the World Trade Center.

Polls conducted by Fox News in July of 2001 indicated that as many as forty-four percent of the nine hundred voters questioned believed Condit was involved in the disappearance of Chandra. Of these, twenty-seven percent felt he needed to resign from his position, while fifty-one percent believed him to be acting as though he were guilty. A similar poll taken from Condit's own district returned slightly more favorable impressions, but months later he would lose the Democratic primary election for his seat in Congress. His former aide, Dennis Cardoza took over his position, and Condit's involvement in the disappearance of Chandra Levy was cited as a chief concern among voters.

The case began to return fewer leads. A grand jury assembled to quiz Condit on his involvement, but the date was to remain a strict secret. Already annoyed by the leaks to the press of his involvement, Condit wanted his appearance to be kept quiet. The Congressman's term would eventually finish at the beginning of 2003, and he would leave his office.

Solving the Case

During May of 2002, investigators announced they had discovered the remains of a human. The skeleton was found by a dog walker who had paused to look for turtles in Rock Creek Park. The Police Chief, Charles Ramsey, announced that investigators had followed up the man's report by finding bones and personal effects that had been left around a secluded, forested area. They had not been buried. Among the personal items found were tennis shoes, a sweat shirt, athletic leggings, and a sports bra, all of which were recovered by detectives. The zone was not included in the original search due to its remoteness and the difficulty of accessing the area, which was close to a mile from the Pierce-Klingle Mansion and roughly four miles from Chandra's home.

Following a preliminary autopsy, the police investigators confirmed the remains were those of Chandra Levy, and announced that enough evidence was present to launch a homicide case. A more complete autopsy carried out in May confirmed the death as being the result of murder. Among the evidence for homicide was the damage to specific parts of the skeleton, a clue suggesting that the killer might have strangled the victim. But with such scant evidence and remains available, the doctors confessed that they might never be able to tell for certain exactly what caused the death. In addition to what was recovered by the police, a private investigator searching through the area recovered a shin bone. The additional evidence was around twenty-five yards from the original site and was found by a man the Levy family had hired to investigate Chandra's death. Police described this extra recovery as "unacceptable," lamenting the fact that police had not recovered the shin bone themselves.

In 2002, the family organized a memorial service to be held back in their home town of Modesto, California. Over one thousand people attended the ceremony, which lasted for an hour and a half. The remains would be buried a year later, with Chandra's final resting place being chosen as Lakewood Memorial Park Cemetery in California. The private ceremony saw only forty people in attendance, mainly those who were close to the family. At the culmination of the funeral, the release of a dozen white doves marked the close of the ceremony.

The investigation was still having difficulty. Perhaps the biggest lead had arrived in September of 2001, just when the world was distracted by the events in New York. Investigators had received contact from a man held in a Washington jail who claimed that he possessed pertinent information regarding the death of Chandra Levy. The informant's identity was kept a strict secret out of safety concerns, but his information pointed directly at a man named Ingmar Guandique as being heavily involved in the case. Ingmar Guandique was a twenty-year-old immigrant from El Salvador, being held in prison for assaulting a pair of women in the same park where the remains of Chandra Levy had been found. According to the informant, Ingmar Guandique claimed to have been paid twenty-five thousand dollars to kill Chandra. Despite this information, police ruled out the potential involvement of Condit and the idea that he may have paid to have his young lover killed, based on the fact that Ingmar Guandique had already assaulted women in the very same park. Coupled with this, he had failed to arrive at his place of work on the day of the murder. A testimony from Guandique's landlady suggested that he had arrived home that same night with cuts and scratches along his face. However, Guandique's other victims were not interviewed. Charles Ramsey, the police chief leading the investigation, refused to classify Ingmar Guandique as a suspect, instead referring to him as a "person of interest." He requested that media reporters should not make a big deal about the involvement of Ingmar Guandique in the killing of Chandra Levy.

Separate from the investigation, Ingmar Guandique was sent to prison for the assaults he had committed on two women in Rock Creek Park. When asked about Chandra, he denied being involved. Investigating further, the FBI decided to have their informant take a polygraph test. He failed. A similar test carried out on Guandique ruled that the answers he provided were "not deceptive." Due to the fact that both men spoke very little English, police investigators commented that they would have preferred a bi-lingual person to have carried out the test. Such a person was unavailable at the time. The judge who sentenced Ingmar Guandique for his assaults was asked about the involvement of the man in the case of Chandra Levy, but the judge dismissed the matter as a "satellite issue." Guandique received ten years in jail for assaulting the two women at Rock Creek Park. Without any further leads, Chandra's case was officially deemed to be cold.

The murder would remain a cold case until 2006. During this time, Charles Ramsey was succeeded by Cathy Lanier as the chief of police in Washington D.C. She appointed three veteran homicide investigators to take over the case. As well as this, in 2007, the Washington Post appointed a team of reporters to re-evaluate the information available to them about the case. From here, the newspaper began to publish a series of stories (in 2008) connecting the failures of the police department in connecting Ingmar Guandique to the crime. Acting on the renewed interest, a search of Guandique's prison cell recovered a photograph of Chandra that had been saved from a magazine. The detectives appointed to the case began to interview acquaintances and associates of Ingmar Guandique, as well as the witnesses in the cases of assault for which he had been imprisoned.

The Trial

This work led the team to issue a warrant for the arrest of Ingmar Guandique in March of 2009, eight years after the original crime. After a few days switching between custody and being interviewed by a series of officers, Ingmar Guandique was charged with the murder of Chandra Levy. A grand jury indicted him on six counts:

1. Kidnapping
2. First degree murder committed during a kidnapping
3. Attempted first degree sexual abuse
4. First degree murder committed during a sexual offense
5. Attempted robbery
6. First degree murder committed during a robbery

Despite the charges, Guandique pleaded not guilty. His trial was set for January 2010. One argument made by his lawyers suggested that the jail cell was not within the jurisdiction of a search warrant issued by the court. This, coupled with the contamination of several pieces of DNA evidence, meant that the trial was rescheduled for the following October.

Selection of jury members began in October of 2010 in the Superior Court of the District of Columbia. The potential witnesses put forward by the U.S. Attorney included an FBI agent who had worked on the case and the two women whom Guandique had been convicted of assaulting in the Park. Initial forecasts for the trial set the time for the prosecution at four weeks and the time estimated for the defense was just one day. On the twenty-fifth and twenty-sixth of October, the women testified about the time they had been assaulted by Guandique. Both had been jogging in the same Park where Chandra's remains had been found. One testimony included the details that Guandique had grabbed the woman from behind and then dragged her down into a ravine while holding a knife against her face.

Also testifying was Robert Levy, Chandra's father. Sixty-four years old at the time of the trial, he began to refute statements he had made regarding his suspicion of Congressman Condit in the murder. He told the court room that during the early years of the investigation, he had suspected that Condit had been involved and that Chandra would have been too cautious to be running alone in the woods. He no longer believed this to be true. Another refutation involved the idea he had given to police that Chandra and Condit had shared a five-year plan for their futures, involving their eventual marriage. Levy confessed to saying whatever came into his head regarding Condit involvement in the case. At the time, he had wished to paint the Congressman as the villain in the piece. His mind was changed, he told the court, when he learned of the involvement of Ingmar Guandique. The Congressman took to the stand himself. Condit was asked on three separate occasions about the nature of the relationship between himself and Chandra. He refused to respond, citing the privacy of both himself and the murdered girl. An FBI biologist who did testify told the court of the DNA match between sperm found on Chandra's underwear and the Congressman's own DNA profile.

One of the key testimonies for the prosecution came from Armando Morales, the man who shared a cell with Ingmar Guandique in Kentucky. He mentioned Guandique being concerned about having to transfer between prisons due to the hostility and violence shown by other inmates towards those who had committed rape. Both men were members of the Mara Salvatrucha gang. When confiding in Morales, Guandique had confessed to having killed Chandra Levy while attempting to steal from her. Despite this confession, Guandique remained resolute that he had not raped the woman.

Two of the charges (sexual assault and murder associated with that assault) were dropped by the prosecution on the 10th of November as they rested their case. The defense chose not to call Ingmar Guandique to the stand. A selection of prison inmates were called up by the defense and began to refute the testimony given by Morales. One, Jose Manuel Alaniz, suggested that there had been no mention of rape or murder during the time the group shared the cell in Kentucky. While being cross-examined, however, Alaniz did admit that he had wished to refrain from appearing too "nosy" and had spent a large amount of time asleep, recovering from a bullet wound. A further two charges were dropped by the prosecution due to the statute of limitations expiring, meaning

Ingmar Guandique was no longer being prosecuted for either kidnapping or armed robbery.

The remaining charges were first degree murder committed during a kidnapping and during a robbery. It was the prosecution's assertion that Guandique had bound and gagged Chandra Levy before leaving her to die of exposure and dehydration in the park. To counter this point, the defense reiterated the lack of DNA evidence linking Guandique to the scene of the crime. While labelling the case against Ingmar Guandique as "fiction," the defense posited the theory that Chandra had been murdered elsewhere and had then been dumped in the park. The jury retired.

It took two days for the jury to almost reach a verdict. All members but one returned a guilty plea. On the third day, the jury requested that the judge clarify the definition of assault as it pertained to the case. The judge responded with the assertion that assault could technically be any injury, no matter how small it might be. After two more days of deliberation, the jury returned a verdict in which they voted unanimously to convict Ingmar Guandique. When asked about the verdict after the trial, a member of the jury mentioned that the testimony of Morales had played a key role in the group reaching their decision.

For some, the verdict was described as "miraculous," due to the reaching of a guilty verdict despite there being only circumstantial evidence. Despite the case going cold for a number of years, the case had been eventually solved using only a small amount of evidence. Gladys Weatherspoon, who had represented Ingmar Guandique during his earlier assault charges, confessed that she was worried by the jury's verdict and the fact that they had always seemed destined to reach a decision of guilty. She mentioned the presence of Chandra's mother in the courtroom as causing the jury to feel sorry for the family. After the trial, the Levy family held a press conference in which they admitted that, despite the verdict, there was no sense of closure regarding the death of their daughter.

Because of the nature of the jury's decision, an appeal always seemed to be likely. In February of 2011, Ingmar Guandique's lawyers requested that there be a retrial, citing their suspicion that the verdict had not been attained in the proper manner. they put together a seventeen-page report detailing their issues with the case, including claims that the prosecution team had made appeals to the emotions of the case, rather than the facts, and that one juror (who had taken no notes during the trial) had referred to the notes of another juror, despite the judge's instructions that this would not be allowed. The team for the prosecution opposed such a move, claiming that the issue regarding the notes was simply a technical issue and held no significant effect on the jury reaching a final verdict.

Ingmar Guandique faced the possibility of spending thirty years to life in jail. At most, he would be imprisoned for life without the possibility of parole. This was the sentence sought by the prosecution, who said that Guandique was always unable to control himself and that he would always pose a significant threat to women. A memo was submitted to the courts before sentencing, mentioning Guandique's harassment of female prison staff. An American attorney was also dispatched to El Salvador to investigate Guandique's criminal past. They suspected he had been forced to flee the country because of his attacks against women.

With sentencing due to begin on the 11th of February, 2011, Ingmar Guandique said to the family of Chandra Levy that he was sorry for what had happened to their daughter but continued to maintain his innocence. Chandra's mother demanded an answer from Guandique. She asked him directly whether he was the one who killed her daughter, demanding that the suspect look her in the eye and tell her. It did not happen...

Any motions requesting a retrial were denied, and instead Guandique received sixty years in jail. In a closing statement, the judge remarked that Guandique would remain a danger to women and others for some time and described him as a sexual predator. Throughout, the accused protested his innocence.

Current Status

Over the coming years, it was still not entirely possible to put the cold case to bed. Despite the murder of Chandra Levy being committed in 2001, grand juries and courts discussed the case through the early 2010s. Occasional evidence came to surface and occasional claims were made for a retrial. Often, the media was not given details of the court's decisions in each instance. For many, the case of Chandra Levy had reached a satisfying conclusion with the imprisonment of Ingmar Guandique.

But that is not where this story ends. As recently as May 2015, prosecutors have abandoned their opposition to Ingmar Guandique receiving a retrial. A new witness found by the defense has led to new evidence coming to light. A neighbor of Chandra's placed a phone call to the emergency services on the last day Chandra was reported alive. She recalls hearing a "blood-curdling scream" coming from an area that may have included Chandra Levy's apartment. Despite the case being closed, this cold case could see further developments in coming years. It just goes to show, it is often impossible to truly consider a case as closed, cold or suitably solved, even after a conviction.

Robert Peterson, Anton Schuessler, and John Schuessler

Where: Chicago

When: October, 1955

Suspect(s): Silas Jayne, Kenneth Hansen

Date of conviction: 2002

Background Information

Our next case is slightly shorter. Rather than one murder, it involves the disappearance of three people at the hands of one man. The vanishing of Robert Peterson, Anton Schuessler, and John Schuessler became a famous case in the 1950s. Despite the media circus and interest surrounding the event, it would be fifty years before it was solved. Despite the five decades worth of time passing between the original crime and the conviction, we are still missing some of the facts that eluded detectives and investigators for half a century. More importantly, the case involved one of Chicago's most notorious criminals, Silas Jayne. To fully understand the case, it is important to learn exactly how Silas was positioned in the contemporary society.

Silas Carter Jayne was born in 1907, the son of a farmer in Illinois. There were eleven children in the family, and Silas was the eldest of the boys. Silas's first criminal conviction arrived in 1924, when he was aged just seventeen. He served a year in jail after raping a girl. Following his release, he began to work closely with his brothers, returning to the family's Chicago-based stables, named the Green Tree Stables. There was also an academy attached to the premises, where young people learned how to ride. The brothers found success in their horse trade attempts, working their way up to owning a ranch near Woodstock. Here, they would move the feral horses they took from the West of America all the way to the Illinois rail works.

During this time, Silas Jayne began to get a reputation as something of a bully. Despite this, he was well regarded for his business acumen when it came to the world of horses. Due to his previous conviction for rape, Silas was exempt from the draft instituted during the Second World War. Instead, he traded in horse meat. Using the profits from this side of the business, he began to move into the top end of the equestrian world, running a stable often used by those in the elite world of Chicago show horses. A favorite trick was to convince the daughters of rich men to purchase horses of little real value, convincing them that these were the best available, the kind of horse they might need if they were to succeed in the riding championships.

With a reputation as a heavy drinking, gruff man, Silas Jayne was noted for his rough speaking and sometimes overbearing approach. Despite this, it was standard practice for parents to leave their young daughters with the stables for extended lengths of time. It was a common boast from Jayne to his associates that he had molested many of the young girls entrusted to his care, almost all of whom were underage. Following the complaints regarding the poor quality of horses Jayne had sold to many of the fathers, Jayne would inform the fathers of their daughters' notoriously promiscuous reputation among his employees. Worried about potential scandals erupting, the fathers would often back away from their complaints and found it unworthy of their time to press Silas Jayne too hard.

Many of the allegations made against Silas Jayne were not investigated. For some, the reason can be put down to the friendly relationship Jayne shared with the local police force. As well as this, he had various ties to the local organized crime rings. Though not a mobster himself, Jayne's stables were used by people such as "Mad Sam" DeStefano and other members of the mob. It has been suggested that the various gangsters would arrive at Jayne's Idle Hour Stables to ride around on the horses and "play cowboy" by firing their guns into the air. At the age of eighty, Silas Jayne died of leukemia. The year was 1987. But why has his name been included in the list of cold cases?

Discovering the Bodies

To find out more, we must go to the year of 1955. On the 18th of October, three naked bodies were discovered in a ditch on the northwest side of Chicago. They belonged to Robert Peterson, Anton Schuessler, and John Schuessler, aged fourteen, eleven, and thirteen respectively. The ditch was located in the Robinson Forest Preserve. When they were found, the boys had been missing for two days. The three had been travelling from Jefferson Park all the way downtown in order to visit the cinema and watch Walt Disney's "The African Lion." After the discovery of the bodies, very little progress was made. No arrests and no convictions meant that the case became one of Chicago and America's most notorious cold cases.

The Investigation

It would be forty years before a proper investigation could reach a conclusion. In 1977, ATF agents began to investigate the disappearance of Helen Brach, the heiress to Brach's candy. Through their investigations, they came across a man known as Kenneth Hansen. They learned from their informants that Hansen had been heard to boast of murdering the boys. He had even threatened to other people that they would end up suffering from the same fate. A similar story originated from an informant in the 1970s, but the FBI took no action at the time.

Hansen had been twenty-two years old at the time of the murder. He had met with the boys while they had been hitchhiking across the town. The last time anyone had seen them alive was when they had been spotted by a classmate at a bowling alley close to eight miles from the theatre they were hoping to visit. From here, Hansen had lured the boys into the Idle Hours stables, pretending that he was taking them to show them the horses. Here, he began sexually abusing the Schuessler boys and was discovered by Robert Peterson. On being discovered, Hansen attacked and killed all three.

Silas Jayne had discovered the truth about the murders. Believing that the murders might be enough to destroy his business and bring his own crimes to light, Jayne covered up the crime. He had the bodies loaded into a station wagon and taken to the woods for disposal. This would be where they were eventually found. This movement matched up with predictions made by the original forensic investigators, who noted the marks on the boys' bodies as being similar to those caused by floor mats in such a vehicle. In 1956, the barn where the murders had taken place burned down. Authorities believed it to be a case of arson.

It emerged that the police had received reports of screams coming from the stables on the day the boys had disappeared. These leads had not been followed up, in spite of the stables' close proximity to the place the bodies had been found. One detective who worked on the case recalled how Kenneth Hansen had been suspected to have preyed on hundreds of boys before being arrested in 1995. At this point, he was convicted for murdering the three children. This information likely led to the courts overturning the trial verdict five years later, suggesting that the jury should not have been privy to the prejudicial testimony as it pertained to Hansen's predilection for cruising the streets of Chicago in search of young boys. There was a retrial in 2002, and the verdict was ratified. Hansen was, at last, found guilty. He would die in 2007.

For many people, however, this cold case is not simply dependent on Hansen being tracked down for the murder of the three boys. Instead, the real concern is the involvement of Silas Jayne in covering up the crime. Despite this one case taking fifty years to reach a satisfying conclusion, it was not the only one involving Jayne.

The Prime Suspect

As well as the murder of the three boys, it is suspected that Silas Jayne was heavily involved in the disappearance of Ann Miller, Patricia Blough, and Renee Bruhl. The three women were last seen in 1966, boarding a boat similar to the one owned by someone who worked at the stables possessed by Jayne. Two of the women had roomed their own horses at Jayne's stables and were suspected to have been witnesses to the bombing of Cheryl Lynn Rude in 1965. They were never seen again, and their case remains unsolved.

Similarly, Silas Jayne's attempts to have his brother George killed were known to the police. He had contracted a number of hit teams to carry out the task. One team hired in 1965 turned around and told George about the impending assassination, and George convinced them to go to the police. An investigation nearly trapped Silas, with an undercover officer posing as a potential hit man. Despite this, the 1966 trial ended in Silas Jayne's acquittal. The state's key witness contracted a sudden, debilitating case of amnesia and was unable to even recall what he had eaten for breakfast that morning. George was eventually shot in the heart in 1970 while playing cards with his family.

The Conviction

Silas Jayne was ultimately convicted of conspiracy to commit murder in 1973. He served seven years in jail. Until Hansen's trial at the turn of the century, his involvement in the death of the three boys was limited only to rumors and suggestions. For those who were investigating criminal cases in Chicago in the 1950s and 1960s, the figure of Silas Jayne loomed large. Thought to be involved in a string of other incidents, the truth about Silas Jayne might be what is preventing us from closing yet more cold cases. In this instance, however, we were able to catch the criminal who killed the three boys in Chicago.

Lucy Johnson

Where: Vancouver, Canada
When: 1961
Suspect: N/A
Date of conviction: N/A

Background Information

Not all cold cases are murders. For some, the true tragedy of a cold case is in not knowing whether a family member is alive or dead. When no remains are found and when no trail of clues exists to lead the investigators to the eventual solution, the disappearance of a family member can be absolutely heart-breaking. It can be even worse when the family themselves are suspected of being involved. One such case is that of Lucy Johnson.

The Disappearance

Lucy Johnson was first reported as a missing person in 1961, but it took almost a decade for her to be reunited with the young family she left behind, including daughter Linda Evans. Linda was just seven years old when her mother was first reported as missing. It took the police a further three years to receive an official missing person's report. The domestic situation was such that the vanishing of Lucy Johnson from the family home was both expected and unexpected. Few could blame her for leaving of her own accord, but some suspected that she might not have had a say in the matter. As such, the family's garden was excavated by the police detectives investigating Lucy's disappearance. Nothing was ever found, despite the digging up of most of the garden. The young Linda had to look on, unsure of exactly what had happened to her mother.

The Investigation Closing the Case

The case remained cold until many years later. Recently, as part of a retrospective review of numerous cold cases in the area, local police highlighted the disappearance of Lucy Johnson as one they had never been able to solve. To back this up, the ever curious and now adult Linda took out a series of adverts in newspapers across the region in Canada where she knew her mother had roots. Despite not expecting to hear much, Linda received a phone call from a woman who recognized the picture as being that of her own mother. This woman contacted police and contacted Linda. She would eventually be revealed as Linda's half-sister, a fellow daughter of Lucy Johnson.

Lucy Johnson was still alive. She had fled across the country, away from an abusive husband. After being put in touch with her newly discovered half-sister, Linda made the journey to visit her mother and to discover more about what had caused her to leave the family behind. The most pressing issue she had during the trip was simply the question of why Lucy had left in the first place. For the police back at home, the potential to close the cold case also lay in the same answer.

They were not her only questions. As well as the facts, there were bigger issues: whether mother and daughter would recognize one another, whether the sisters would look alike, and just how Linda would fit into the new group of family her mother had built up around her. Unlike cold cases where there is a murder, the reappearance of a vanished person after so long leads to many people having to navigate emotional issues and confront a great number of realities. Linda admitted that she was reluctant to push the new acquaintances too hard.

For Linda, one of the major issues was that she had assumed her mother to be dead. The sudden realization was, that not only was she alive, but also that Linda was now able to go and visit the woman who had vanished from her life many years ago. She tried to imagine these questions existing in her mother's mind, but with little experience of the woman outside of childhood, she found it hard to contemplate her mother's potential thoughts, feelings, and reactions.

The Reunion

After fifty-two years apart, however, they recognized one another right away. They met at the airport. Not only was Lucy there, but so was Linda's half-sister, her half-brother, and numerous aunts. They were all waiting for her to arrive. Upon seeing one another, Lucy ran towards her daughter, took her in her arms, and immediately told her, "I love you." The two half-sisters looked alike, sharing their fair skin and freckles. This helped her mother spot her long-lost daughter straight away. After the initial contact, the group retreated to a nearby coffee shop. Once the buoyed effect of the instant recognition had worn off, conversation was a little bit stilted and awkward, as should be expected after so long apart.

For Linda, the constant source of amazement was her mother's face. They had been apart for fifty-two years, and Linda had assumed her mother to be dead. Sitting in a coffee shop and then travelling home with her was somewhat of a surreal experience. Aside from the emotions, she could see traces of her own appearance in her mother and in the extended family. There still remained the most pressing issue, however, one which continued to bother Linda. Now that she knew her mother was alive, Linda needed to know what had caused her mother to leave. Linda was sure that she would not be able to leave her own children the way her mother had done. She needed answers.

These answers would arrive on the second day. Linda was there for a week to visit, but after one day of bottling up her thoughts, she allowed herself to ask the most pressing questions on the second day. She asked Lucy why she had left and why she had become a cold case file without even so much as a hint of communication in the ensuing years.

Lucy responded with a story that might have been all too familiar in the 1950s. She was stuck in an abusive relationship, Linda's father not only abusing Lucy, but also openly cheating on her with other women. After she tried to leave, and after Linda's father told her to leave, she had returned for the children. However, her husband said that she would never take them. She could leave in peace, but she would never be able to take the kids. Never again would she try to extricate the children from their home.

Linda didn't know whether to take the story at face value or whether to think parts were exaggerated. Without any way of checking the story, she decided to simply let it go. Though she confessed to still doubting parts of the story, she did not want to. If anything, she knew that Lucy wanted her daughter to believe the story. That was enough.

Unfortunately, the reunion was not an entirely happy meeting. While Linda was keen to reunite with her long lost family, she brought with her some bad news. In the fifty-two years that had passed, her brother, Lucy's first son, had passed away. After a week together, Linda departed from her newly found mother, leaving her with the news of her first son's death, but leaving her also with the newfound relationships the pair had formed.

The case itself is no longer cold. Rather than having to chalk it up as another unsolved murder, the police were able to instead determine that Lucy Johnson was alive and well. The time they had spent digging up and excavating the yard was time wasted. Across the country, Lucy had been starting a new life. For the family she left behind – now just Linda – the discovery of a real person at the end of a telephone line brings with it a flood of emotions. As well as the satisfaction of learning what exactly happened all those years ago, she now knows she can pick up the phone and speak to her mother at any time. As it turns out, not all cold cases have a sad ending.

Minnie and Ed Maurin

Where: Chehalis, Wa
When: December 1985
Suspect: Ricky A. Riffe
Date of conviction:

Background Information

Sometimes, the real issue with a cold case is amassing the evidence required to prove what everybody already knows. At certain points in a case, the identity of the killer can be clear to all of those involved, including the detectives, the family of the victims, the press, the public, and everyone else. However, these suspicions are often difficult to prove. Modern court systems depend on the model of innocent until proven guilty and always need to have the case proved beyond a reasonable doubt. While this can often offer protection to the falsely accused, it can be a real hindrance to cases that have gone cold. Trying to find that one missing piece of evidence, the smoking gun that points at the accused can be very hard. When it finally comes to surface, however, it can be all the more satisfying.

In the case of Minnie and Ed Maurin, people suspected that Ricky A. Riffe was the man behind their murder for many years. It took almost two decades to prove beyond immeasurable doubt, however, that he was the one who killed the couple.

The Disappearance

The case begins on the 19th of December 1985. Investigations found that Ed Maurin withdrew eight and a half thousand dollars in one hundred dollar bills that evening. He had visited the bank in Chehalis to make his withdrawal. This would be the last time he would be seen alive. The very next day, just five days before Christmas, the couple's car was found abandoned at a nearby shopping center. It was covered in blood, but no bodies were present.

A large manhunt took place. Detectives and volunteers scoured the local countryside searching for any remains or clues to the whereabouts of the Maurins. It took almost a week for the pair to be found. Their bodies were discovered on Christmas Day. From the evidence that the medical examiners and autopsies were able to gather, it seems they were each shot in the back while they sat in their car. Their bodies were dumped and the car moved. The bodies were found just a short distance away from a logging area near Adna. Though the elderly couple's bodies were found on Christmas Day, 1985, the case to find their killer was not successful.

The Investigation

For many, the key culprit was Ricky Riffe, whom many suspected to be somehow involved in the killings. But, in spite of the wide-held belief of his involvement, there was no way of putting together a complete case against Ricky. The murders went unpunished. Annoyed by the lack of closure, the family took it upon themselves to ensure the case never went too cold. Despite the police all but gave up on it, the family grouped together and hired themselves a pair of private investigators.

Though it would still be a decade before the private investigation bore fruit, the tireless work of the private detectives led to a number of new witnesses coming forward and giving evidence about the case. Their accounts formed the backbone of a renewed effort to put the right man behind bars, and their details were passed along to the sheriff's department. From here, Ricky Riffe was arrested and put on trial. Now fifty-five years old, he had been a young man when the murders had originally taken place. He had moved to a place named King Salmon in Alaska but was forced to return to Lewis County to stand trial for his crimes. At this point, the police admitted that both Ricky and his brother had been suspects in the 1990s, but the then prosecution team had been unable (or unwilling) to put together a case. Armed with the new witness testimonies, a case was ready to be made.

One of the most important testimonies came from a man who claimed to have seen both of the Riffe brothers sitting inside the vehicle that belonged to the Maurins on the morning on the 19th of December. Similarly, other eyewitnesses claim to have seen only one man sitting in the back seat of the car that same day.

When presented with a line-up of men, a number of witnesses were able to correctly select the Riffe brothers. It was a well-known fact around the town that the brothers did everything together. The two were known as being inseparable. By the time of the trial, however, John Riffe had already passed away at fifty. As such, the younger brother was unable to be tried for the murder of Minnie and Ed Maurin.

The Trial

It was a short trial, and the jury took only a few hours to reach their decision. They found Ricky Riffe guilty of murder. For the family of those involved, it came as a huge relief. The grandchildren of Ed and Minnie remarked that it was now possible for people to remember their grandparents as people, rather than homicide victims. Two of the couple's children, now both eighty years old, were seated in the front row of the court room, watching the man who had murdered their parents. They had sat there for the whole trial. In spite of their overwhelming relief at the final conviction, one of them did express sympathy for Riffe's family. They also mentioned that they had been sure for two decades that he had been the guilty party. Ever since 1992, he (and presumably others in the town) had been sure that Ricky Riffe and his brother had been involved in the crime. All they lacked was the final piece of proof. The new witness accounts were enough to confirm what everybody had already known. They were enough to take the case out of the cold and seal it for the last time.

The Verdict

In his closing statement, the judge thanked the jury for their ability to reach a quick decision. But he also made a particular effort to thank the detectives who had worked to uncover the new evidence. Finally, he thanked the family for their persistence and for never giving up on the case. Sherry Tibbetts, the partner of Ricky, left the court without so much as sharing a glance with the convicted man. With her was the couple's son.

Not everybody was pleased by the verdict. One local attorney, a man named Sam Groberg, remarked that he regarded the events in court as "appalling" and mentioned that he had never before seen such a huge difference in the testimonies given by witnesses originally and in their final form. Over the course of time, he suggested, their accounts had changed, allowing Ricky to be convicted. Because of the perceived injustice, he admitted that he was committed to helping Ricky get an honest trial. Even if the man were guilty, it was the belief of some that the court and the trial were not fair on the condemned man. With so many assuming Ricky to be guilty and such a huge distance between the original events and the final verdict, reaching an honest conclusion seemed difficult. Despite many being happy that the case is no longer open, there remain doubts over whether it should really have stayed as a cold case.

Helen Sullivan

Where: Long Beach, Ca
When: January, 1972
Suspect: Emanuel Miller
Date of conviction: No conviction – crime solved in 2012

Background Information

It is strange to think of a time when we did not have DNA profiling available to the police investigating any crime. In these modern days, it is not a huge amount of work to simply search through a known database using materials found at the scene or even to match up samples taken from prime suspects against the DNA recovered from a large area. This miraculous technology is perhaps taken for granted and has certainly made it easier to solve crimes in the current day. But what about cold cases? One of the biggest benefits of the technology we now have at our disposal is that it grants us the ability to retrospectively look back over the cases we thought to be unsolvable and to find answers where we thought there might be no chance of ever finding the perpetrator.

The Crime

One such case is the murder of Helen Sullivan. The Long Beach mother of three was sexually assaulted and killed at her home in 1972. Despite being stabbed to death in one of the area's most brutal killings, there has been scant evidence available to track down the killer. At the time, the investigators were left perplexed and unable to crack the case. However, the use of recent federal grant funding in the area has provided the Long Beach Police Department with the opportunity to look back over their unsolved crimes and use modern technology to re-examine some of the most notoriously difficult cases.

Perhaps the most important factor in the ability of the police to return to the Helen Sullivan case was the existence of biological evidence recovered from the scene. At the time, the DNA sequencing technology that is now so common was either unavailable to local police departments or simply not ready for widespread use.

The original crime occurred during the early morning of the 21st of January, 1972. Helen was working late at home, going over her plans for her position as a salesperson for Amway and NutriLite. Her husband was working too, covering the graveyard shift at a local Shell Oil in the nearby area of Wilmington. He would be the first to discover his wife's murder when he came home that night.

The Investigation and Fruitless Conclusion

The investigations into the murder reached no conclusions. Officially a cold case for forty years, the evidence and materials recovered from the scene were placed into storage. As part of the retrospective examination, detectives took the

DNA material and passed it through the database they had at their disposal. It returned a match. Nearly four decades on from the original crime, detectives were led to the profile of one Emanuel Miller.

Emmanuel Miller was a career criminal with a long record of crimes involving sexual assaults against women. In January 1972, he had recently been released from jail in Los Angeles. Detectives believe that Miller may well have been drawn to the area of Helen Sullivan's home due to the large number of empty properties. The arrival of a large-scale freeway construction project in the area had driven many people away. That night, he went to her home and assaulted Helen before killing her. He would escape police attention for forty years.

The case would not reach a conviction, however. Despite the evidence now at the disposal of the police department, Miller's death in 1990 meant that he was far from the clutches of the law. With no one to press charges against, their case remained without a conviction, even if they were to solve the crime.

And in this respect lies one of the biggest difficulties facing those who work on cold cases. The vast expanse of time between the original crime and the time when the case is finally solved means that the on-going lives of those involved never stop. Sometimes it is the detective or the witnesses who meet an untimely end before seeing the case reach its conclusion. Despite this, people still work towards finding the answer for the huge number of cold cases that remain extant.

Colette Aram

Where: Keyworth, Nottinghamshire, Great Britain
When: 30th October 1983
Suspect: Paul Hutchinson
Conviction: 21st December 2009

Background Information

The use of retrospective technology on a variety of cold cases is not limited to America. In Great Britain, the death of Colette Aram became one of the country's most famous cold cases. It would be nearly thirty years before the crime could be solved. Perhaps the most famous aspect of the case was the use of media, which at that time was somewhat revolutionary. A television show called "Crimewatch" was the first of its kind in the United Kingdom, featuring a weekly run down of the country's crimes that the police were particularly struggling to solve. Featuring recreations, information and appeals for witnesses, the show would go on to become an institution. Collete's murder was one of the very first cases to feature on the show, and because of this it became something of a famous case, unsolved for many years.

The Crime

The case begins in the year 1983 on the day before Halloween, the 30th of October. Colette Aram was a sixteen-year-old native of Keyworth in Nottinghamshire, England. She was training to be a hairdresser. That night, she was making the journey from her home to her boyfriend's house. She left her door at just after eight o'clock. The journey was not a long one, a distance of only one and a half miles. Typically, her boyfriend would collect her from her house in his car and the pair would travel together. On this night, however, his car was unavailable. The last time Colette was seen was ten minutes after she had left her home, when she paused to talk to a small group of friends on a nearby road. There have been reports from witnesses that recall hearing a loud scream from a woman quickly followed by the screech of tires as a car sped away at a high speed. No one would ever see Colette alive again.

The alarm was raised that night. Having failed to arrive at her destination, her boyfriend placed a number of phone calls to any place she might have gone. Increasingly frantic, it was half past ten before he rang the police. As well as the authorities, he enlisted the help of friends and family in trying to track her down. The next morning, at nearly nine o'clock, Colette's naked body was discovered. She had been killed and the body dumped in a local field just over a mile from the place she had last been seen. Investigators were able to determine that she had been strangled and raped.

The Investigation

A murder investigation was quickly launched by the police. By the 7th of June, having made little progress, the decision was taken to make Colette's killing the first case to feature on the new British television show, "Crimewatch." The BBC program detailed recent crimes both as a warning to the public and as an appeal for more information. The show featured a reconstruction of the night Colette Aram was killed. It was broadcast at nine o'clock to the whole country. Following the broadcast, the police saw a huge spike in the numbers of witnesses calling in with information. In all, they received close to four hundred pieces of information, allowing them to remove one and a half thousand potential suspects from their enquiry. Despite this newfound wealth of information, they were unable to track down the killer. The case went cold. Its position as the first show on "Crimewatch," as well as it being unsolved, led it to garner something of a reputation. It was featured again in 2004 on the show's 20th anniversary special. As the first case and one which had still not been solved, Colette's murder was included. However, the case remained cold.

Closing the Case

The breakthrough would occur in 2008. Due to advances in DNA technology, it was now possible for the investigating units to assemble a profile of the killer using samples and data they had gathered during the initial investigation. Using this profile, there was an appeal for people in the area to come forward with names of potential suspects. With this information, a swab could be taken of the suspect's mouth and the DNA matched against the profile of the killer. A similar case involving a man known as the M25 rapist (named after a local highway) had been successful using this approach. Over one hundred calls came from the public. The police used this information to assemble a list of the most likely suspects, and they began to take samples.

It was June, 2008 before they were able to match the profile against the right suspect. Jean-Paul Hutchinson was originally arrested because of a motoring incident. The standard DNA swab of his mouth was taken as part of the arrest. When searched against the database, it provided a near exact match against that of the killer of Colette Aram. This proved to be a difficulty. Jean-Paul was only twenty years old at the time of his arrest. The crime had taken place before he was born. But this would still prove to be the break through the police needed.

The police tracked down Jean-Paul's father, Paul Stewart Hutchinson. In 2008, he was fifty years old. His DNA matched that of the killer (the DNA he shared with his son), and he was arrested in April of 2009. Though he initially pleaded not guilty in the months leading up to his trial, Paul changed his plea on the 21st of December 2009 at his pre-trial hearing. He pleaded guilty to the murder.

In January of 2010, Paul Stewart Hutchinson was sentenced to life in jail with a minimum of twenty-five years before he could be considered for parole. Speaking after the sentencing, Colette's mother Jacqui mentioned that the chance to finally see someone convicted for her daughter's murder brought some relief but reiterated the family's desire to know just why it had been Colette who had been killed. This was a question the killer had been and remained unwilling to answer. DNA evidence can reveal much, but it cannot reveal motivations.

A Twist of Fate

The following October, prison officials in Nottingham found Hutchinson unconscious inside his cell. Calling an ambulance, they rushed him to hospital. He died in transit. Following a brief investigation, it was suspected that he had purposefully overdosed on the medicine he received, but the autopsy was not conclusive.

The Aftermath

After the conviction, the BBC ran a special edition of "Crimewatch" to cover the first case that had featured on the show. During the program, many inaccuracies in the reporting of the crime were exposed, especially those regarding the killer's identity. Some had reported that Hutchinson was a psychology graduate, as well as other untrue information about his background. The show laid these rumors to rest. Despite the forty years between the original murder, the original broadcast, and the capture of the perpetrator, interest in the case remained high. In taking a retrospective look at the murder, "Crimewatch" revealed both what fascinates the public about the many unsolved cases around the world and the changes that have been made in the way crimes are investigated.

Thanks to modern technology, even those cases that were thought unsolvable have been successfully followed through to conclusion.

Linda Strait

Where: Plantes Ferry Park, Wa
When: September, 1982
Suspect: Arbie Dean Williams
Conviction: 2006

Background Information

Sometimes, a case going cold can be difficult to investigate simply because the perpetrator is already serving time behind bars for another crime. Due to his absence from the immediate vicinity, it can be easy to overlook the possibility that they might be involved in the crime. One such crime is the murder of Linda Strait in 1982, which took twenty-one years to solve. After becoming a cold case, it was largely the hard work and endurance of Linda's family that kept the crime at the forefront of investigators and police detectives' minds. It ensured that Linda's situation was never entirely far from the authorities' thoughts. This would pay off in 2006 when Arbie Dean Williams was eventually arrested.

The Disappearance

Linda Strait was a child when she was kidnapped. Unlike the situations one might expect for a kidnapping, this was not conducted in the dead of night and in a clandestine manner. Linda was kidnapped in broad daylight, only a few yards from the family home. There were people all around who had not been paying particular attention to the young girl until it was too late. Once she had been abducted, Linda faced a horrific ordeal. Before she was killed, she would be raped and robbed. Once her killer was finished with her, her body was dumped into a nearby river later that night. When looking back on the crime, Linda's own mother found it difficult to explain how a person could simply drop a body into the Spokane River "like a sack of garbage."

The Investigation

Linda's body would be found the next day by a fisherman in the area. She had washed up on the shore near Plantes Ferry Park. From their initial findings, investigators were able to identify all the hallmarks involved in a rape and could tell that Linda's method of murder had been strangulation. Also found near the body was a discarded pillow case. From this, investigators were able to take semen samples. Though they did not know it at the time, this was the piece of evidence that would eventually lead them to the criminal, even if it took longer than they might ever have imagined.

The DNA evidence taken from the pillow case was not as useful in 1982 as it is now. Instead, it was stored with the other evidence in the case while detectives went about their business. However, the case proved to be tougher than they might have imagined. Not only were there very few leads, but those clues that they did possess seemed to lead them nowhere. Despite the time of day and the nearby people to the site of the kidnapping, there were no witnesses who were able to provide any information that was of any particular use. The case was eventually closed without being able to track down Arbie Dean Williams.

A Killer with a Trail of Bodies

During this time, Arbie Williams was not being idle. Rather than being arrested for the murder of Linda Strait, he was in fact continuing his crime spree. In 1983, he was arrested and tried for the kidnapping of two young girls in Spokane Valley. He had lured the eight-year-old school girls into his vehicle by telling them he had misplaced his keys and needed help trying to find them. It is probable that he used a similar method to abduct Linda.

Once he had trapped the girls inside the car, Williams leaned over and shoved them into the floor. He told them to be absolutely quiet. He drove away with the girls in frightened silence. They drove around for hours like this, waiting for the night to get suitably dark. Once he felt the time was right, Williams pulled the car to the side of the road and ordered the girls to remove their clothes. According to the records from his trial, one of the girls did as she was told while the other managed to escape. The one who had remained was to be the real victim. Williams raped her numerous times and then choked her until the girl passed out. Taking her for dead, he ditched he body in a nearby forest and drove away. While Williams had assumed the girl was dead, she was not. The young girl regained consciousness and fled the area, seeking help.

Those who were investigating the case said they had talked to close to a thousand people in their search for Linda's killer. While Williams had been a suspect, he had outright refused to talk to the police. Even after his arrest for his involvement in the kidnapping of the young girls, he refused to talk to police about Linda. To get around this, the investigators sent away the pillow case that had been found near Linda's body. They wanted to test the DNA against that of Arbie Williams. So convinced were they that he might be involved, they sent the case for testing on two occasions, in 1989 and 1998. Both times, the results came back as inconclusive.

Closing the Case

Finally, determined to find their answer, the detectives sent the sample to a private laboratory. By this time, the year was 2003. Close to two decades had passed since the original crime. The testing took a month, but the results finally were able to provide a match between the pillowcase and Arbie Williams. At this point, Williams was just two days away from a parole hearing. Had this gone according to plan, he would be released for the kidnapping and rape he committed in 1983.

When the family of Linda discovered that the case might finally be reopened and solved, they were laying flowers at the grave of their daughter. At this point, Linda's mother recalls that she had almost lost hope that they would ever find the man responsible for killing their daughter. For the past eleven years, she had been unable to even discuss the case. Now, finally, she might be able to get the answers she had been searching for after nearly twenty years. In the years since, Linda's mother had made a promise to confront the man whom she described as the "scum of the Earth" and was determined to look him in the eye.

The Trial

At the age of sixty-two, Arbie Williams pleaded guilty to the second-degree homicide of Linda Strait. During the hearing, he admitted that he had been the one who "killed Miss Strait," only to try and withdraw his plea when the prosecutors began to detail the crime to the court and the judge. At the trial, Linda's mother took to the stand to explain her pain and suffering since that day in 1982. While on the stand, she told Williams exactly what she thought of him, finally telling him that she hoped he would "rot in hell." Though he wanted to rescind his guilty plea, Williams was informed that he would not be able to rescind his signed confession. Debating his actions with himself, he eventually agreed to continue with his guilty plea.

After the trial, Arbie Williams was sentenced to twenty years. Following these two decades of imprisonment, it would be down to the state whether he would eventually be allowed back into the world. By this time, he would have moved past eighty years old, having spent half his life behind bars. Of all the details that emerged regarding the crime during the trial, perhaps the most important question remained unanswered. Despite speaking for a long time during the session, Williams at no point explained why he had chosen to select Linda that day. As she walked home from the store with an order of milk and a home perming kit, he had picked her from the street. Rather than explaining his actions or asking for forgiveness, Williams admitted that he saw no reason for the family to forgive him for his actions. He also admitted that – had it been available – he would have pleaded guilty for the death penalty. He confessed that he was tired of being in prison. He would have twenty long years still ahead of him.

Joan Harrison

Where: Lancashire, Great Britain
When: November, 1975
Suspect: Christopher Smith
Conviction: February 2011

Background Information

As well as being able to make cases against all of those everyone is sure is guilty, the use of retrospective examination of cold cases can be an enlightening method of finding the true criminal. In the case of Joan Harrison, murdered in Great Britain in 1975, everyone was sure that her death was the work of one of the country's most notorious serial killers, the Yorkshire Ripper. As one of the most violent and prolific killers in the history of the United Kingdom, Peter Sutcliffe's reputation as the Yorkshire Ripper was one of pure evil. With the majority of his crimes coming in the same time frame and the same area as the murder of Joan Harrison, it was perhaps no surprise that the public should turn to Sutcliffe as the likely suspect. Forty years after the original murder, however, new investigations into this cold case revealed that in this instance, the Ripper was innocent. Instead, the evidence led the detectives to the door of another man, one whom no one had suspected.

The Crime

The story begins when Joan Harrison was found in a derelict car garage on the 20th of November, 1975. She had been murdered. At a time when the Yorkshire Ripper was causing terror across the north of England, Joan Harrison's death seemed to fit the Ripper's template. She had spent time working as a prostitute (the favored demographic of Ripper victims), and investigators found a single bite mark left on her breast. As well as this, there were several items of jewelry that were missing from the body. These included the two wedding rings that Joan Harrison had accrued across two marriages. She was found in an old and abandoned garage in Preston. Even though this was slightly outside of the normal territory of the Yorkshire Ripper, many instantly assumed that this was the work of that very same serial killer.

The Investigation

Perhaps because of this, her name was simply added to the growing list of women who had been killed by the man who would eventually be revealed as Peter Sutcliffe. The investigation into the Ripper was complicated and often in danger of collapsing. The murders would eventually give birth to a number of cold cases. As well as the work for which Sutcliffe was eventually tried and found guilty, the work of a hoaxer led detectives far away from the real killer.

During the investigation into the man who police assumed had killed this long list of women, a man named John Humble began to distract police efforts. Humble began a campaign of getting in contact with the police and feeding them false information. One of the murders this fake Ripper took credit for was the death of Joan Harrison. The letters he wrote in 1978 mentioned the death of Joan Harrison. Despite little linking the death of Joan to the case, it was enough for her name to now be a default addition to the list of Ripper victims. In addition to this, the traces of saliva taken from the letters belonged to the same blood group as the person who had committed the murder in Preston. For those investigating, this seemed like more than enough evidence.

Unfortunately, Humble's continued efforts in hoaxing the police involved taking credit for the murders while leading investigators further from the real killer, Peter Sutcliffe. One such hoax involved sending a recording to the police bragging about the killings. In examining the tape, police decided that a certain regional accent was the one they were looking for. The Wearside accent they thought they were searching for was a long distance from both the Preston location of Joan Harrison's murder and the actual location of the real Ripper. By the time the real Ripper was caught, he had killed thirteen women. After police had eventually deduced that the Humble communications were a hoax, that case, too, would go cold. That was, until 2006 when John Humble was caught and charged with perverting the course of justice. His actions had delayed the capture of the real killer and perverted efforts to catch the real killer of Joan Harrison, whom Sutcliffe denied killing. Humble was jailed for eight years. It seemed that Joan's death would never be solved.

Closing the Case

However, DNA evidence would once again come to the rescue. The DNA taken from the scene of Joan's murder was stored in the databases. In 2008, it returned a match. That match belonged to Christopher Smith, originally from Leeds, who was now sixty years old. He had been arrested for driving under the influence of alcohol, and a swab of his saliva was taken as a standard operating procedure. Smith had a long criminal record, involving assault, theft, and a number of different sex attacks. This saliva swab turned up a match against the killer of Joan Harrison.

A Twist of Fate

Before the police could move to arrest their new suspect, however, they faced a new difficulty. Christopher Smith had been suffering from a terminal illness. Before they could arrest him – and just six days after taking the sample – Smith died. The police force had enough evidence to charge him with the murder had he been alive. During a search of his home, investigators discovered a letter written to Smith's family in the days before he passed. In the three page note, Smith decided that he wanted to "set the record straight." He mentioned that he had "lived with it" for close to twenty years and admitted to being "truly sorry" for the pain he caused. He reiterated his love for his family, including his grandchildren and his daughter, but confessed that he could not return to prison. He begged for God's forgiveness and apologized.

Despite not directly admitting to the murder, many have taken it as a confession that he was the man who killed Joan Harrison and that the letter was him coming to terms with the guilt the murder had left in him ever since.

From what has been learned since the death, police have suggested that Smith did not know his victim. Instead, he may have come across her by random chance after being released from a stint in a local prison. The investigators have attributed the arrest to advances in DNA technology since the time of the original murder. By adding this to other evidence they acquired, they felt they had more than enough to convict Chris Smith. After twenty years, the murder of Joan Harrison was revealed to be the work of one man rather than the actions of a serial killer. While he may not have been convicted for his crimes, the letter Smith left behind demonstrates, at least, the extent to which the murder had haunted him for two decades.

Susan Schwarz

Where: Lynnwood, Seattle
When: October, 1979
Suspect: Unknown
Conviction: 2011

Background Information

Trying to solve a cold case is not just a matter of throwing all the DNA samples against the wall until you find the right answer. While these technology advances have been an incredible boon for those investigating the cases presumed to be dead, there also has to be a determination to find the right answer. In the case of Susan Schwartz, detectives introduced a novel method of returning to the cases everyone had assumed to be unsolvable.

The Crime

Susan Schwartz was murdered on the October 22nd, 1979. She had been both strangled and shot while in her house in Lynnwood. As a small city just fifteen miles to the north of Seattle, there was not a huge amount of coverage of the death. Despite the violent nature of the murder, few clues had been left behind. The case was deemed cold for all of thirty-two years.

Voices from Behind the Bars

This was until detectives in Seattle devised a system for dealing with all of the cold cases that had begun to pile up over the decades. They made a deck of playing cards with a cold case, assigned to each of the fifty-two cards. This deck of cold cases had rewards for the arrests and information that might lead to a conviction. By the time Susan's case had been solved, three others had already been cracked using the method. These playing cards were then circulated to the public and especially in the local prisons. Any prisoners who had information pertaining to the cases might be able to curry favor with the authorities if their information led to an arrest.

With many criminals in the prisons known to be associates of those involved in crimes in the Washington area, common sense dictated that those behind bars would be likely to know something about the cases in the deck. In this instance, the case of Susan Schwartz was assigned to the Queen of Hearts. Detectives at the time had a number of suspects in mind but had been unable to make any arrests at the time. However, after circulating the cards, information came to the surface which would eventually lead the authorities to the right man.

This tip came from inside the prison system. The exact details behind the tip were not detailed (perhaps to retain the convict's identity and to preserve their safety). Though we don't know exactly what the prisoner said to detectives, there are a few salient facts that we can put together to learn more about the solving of the case. In all, the new information is likely to arrive in the form of a new witness, someone who is able to place certain people at certain places during the murder.

The Investigation

The case involved evidence being sent to a state-owned criminal laboratory for assessment and testing. This means that it is likely that DNA evidence was involved at this point, probably taken from a new suspect and matched against the evidence gathered from the crime scene. Next, the investigators took to their old files and gathered together as many of the original witnesses as they could. This is likely for the purpose of matching up new stories against the old ones.

One of the key witnesses could well be Mary. Mary was the wife of the suspect and the best friend of Susan. Mary was involved in an abusive relationship and is said to have lived in fear for her life at this point. Worried about the condition of her friend, Susan supposedly began to try and convince Mary that she should leave her relationship and get away for her own good. According to reports from a detective involved in the case, Mary was very young at the time and had suffered physical abuse at the hands of the man who would later be the chief suspect. She had refused to testify during initial investigations, perhaps out of fear.

Closing the Case

Another one of the key witnesses in the case was Susan's father, Henry. He possessed knowledge of the extent to which Susan disliked Mary's husband and that she was planning on telling Mary how to best extricate herself from the situation. This suggests that Henry may well have known who the killer was throughout the years. However, without the right evidence, the investigators were unable to build a satisfactory case against the murderer. Eventually, Mary did leave her husband. Whether she was the witness at the time of the murder is not established.

Rather than Mary, it could have been an associate of her husband who witnessed the murder of Susan Schwartz, who had come to confront Mary's husband or had come in search of Mary. The information that came from the playing cards passed around the prisons was enough to lead police to the killer but the information that they garnered from the case is yet to be made public. It might be that, after all these years, Mary was finally willing to come forward. It might be that the associate of Mary's husband was in jail and was willing to sell out his friend in order to reduce his own sentence. It might even be a simple tip that sent detectives down an entirely different path. Whatever the truth might be, we do not yet know.

Rather than the particular details of this case, the most important and interesting aspect is simply the manner in which the detectives went about solving it. By using their playing cards, they were able to create a simple and easy method of disseminating a large amount of information quickly. As well as Susan's death, this recent endeavor has already led to the solving of three cold cases. There are perhaps many more in the pipeline. With so many such cases across America – and indeed, the world – perhaps it will become a common sight to see a number of localized versions of the playing card system being used in future cold case investigations.

Numerous victims of the BTK killer

Where: Across Kansas
When: 1974–2000
Suspect: Dennis Rader
Date of conviction: February 25, 2005

Background Information

Not all cold cases are one-off incidents that are difficult to track. In some circumstances, a criminal might commit a series of heinous crimes but still manage to evade capture. In all, Dennis Rader killed ten people, but it would not be until close to thirty years after the first attack that he would be arrested. Perhaps due to the commitment of the police involved and perhaps due to the killer's urge to taunt his investigators, Dennis Rader was eventually caught. To know the true story of Rader's criminal history, we should perhaps start at the beginning.

The Making of a Criminal

As the oldest of the four sons in his family, Dennis was the son of Dorothy and William Rader. He was born in Kansas and spent the majority of his childhood in Wichita. There are scant details about his early life, apart from the stories revolving around his possible torture of animals. As a classic childhood trait of many serial killers, it is often one of the pieces of evidence people use when classifying Rader's crimes. As well as this, he demonstrated a sexual fetish for the underwear of women and acted out on this by stealing the various garments (which he would later wear himself) from his victims.

As he moved into adulthood, Rader took the decision to join the Air Force. He spent four years with the military before being discharged. After leaving, he moved to a Wichita suburb. Here, he spent time working in the meat section of a local supermarket. His mother worked as a bookkeeper at the same store. He began to attend a local college and worked towards an associate degree. He studied electronics before enrolling in Wichita State University. He would graduate in 1979 with a bachelor's degree in the administration of justice. From here, he met and married a woman named Paula Dietz, and the pair had two children.

After settling down with his family, Rader held a number of positions. He worked as an assembler for the Coleman Company who supplied outdoor items. Later, he spent fourteen years working at the office a security services company. In this position, he was trusted to install the security systems and alarms in many houses. As such, he often spent time installing security systems for people who were terrified of the murders he was committing. After leaving this position, he took on the role of dogcatcher in Park City, Wichita. Many of the local residents commented on the over-zealous approach he took to the position. Regarded as a very strict person, there were even complaints from people who felt he had put down their dog for no real reason. He stayed in this job until 2005, when the city terminated his contract. He had failed to report for work for several days and had failed to phone in to tell anyone where he was. He had been arrested five days earlier.

In addition to his work history, Rader was a long-standing member of his local Christian community. He attended a Lutheran Church and was even elected into the position of President of the church council. He led a local Cub Scout group. After his arrest in 2005, the judge who oversaw his wife's request for divorce waived the usual sixty-day waiting period and granted her request immediately. At that point, the pair had been married for thirty-five years. During much of this time, Dennis Rader had been killing people.

A Life of Crime

All of the known victims of Dennis Rader died in Kansas. In all, there were ten known victims. He collected trophies and items from the scene of each crime. As well as those who were killed by Rader, there were numerous others who had somehow escaped his intentions. One of these was Anna Williams, a sixty-three-year-old woman. In 1979, she would escape Rader's clutches by returning to her home much later than she was scheduled. During his confession, Rader mentioned being infuriated by this. He had become obsessed with the woman and had been waiting in her home for hours. Instead, she had been visiting friends. She was one of the lucky ones. At the time of his arrest, Rader admitted that he had planned to kill again. But how did he escape from the authorities for so long and how did the case go so cold?

One of the main features of Rader's campaign of terror was his penchant for sending letters to the local media and police departments. During the five years after 1974, he would write a number of letters. The first to be sent was hidden inside a book and placed inside a public library in Wichita. The letter provided vivid details of the killing of an entire family in January of 1974. To back up this first letter, he wrote again in 1978, sending his message to a local television station. As well as demanding recognition for his crimes, he posited a variety of nicknames. Of all those listed, one stuck. BTK. Announcing himself as a serial killer who planned to kill again, he finished the letter by rewriting a classic American folk song, replacing the lyrics with his own morbid version.

There was much discussion surrounding the Fager family's death. They lived in Wichita, and all three were killed in 1988. Another letter was sent to the police claiming that the deaths were not the work of BTK. The writer did, however, state that he admired the work. Police were able to prove in 2005 that Rader had not written the letter or committed the crime. Such was his reputation by this point, however, that people were willing to believe he had.

In the ensuring thirty years, the case grew cold. Rader's actions were sporadic and always carefully planned. His communications with the media had also slowed and had proved to be untraceable. This was to be the case until 2004, when Rader resumed his efforts to communicate under the guise of BTK. While other cold cases might involve continued hard work on behalf of the investigators, in this instance, it was the hubris of the murderer that led to his capture. The eleven communications made by Rader at this point led to him being caught.

One of the first letters was sent in 2004. It was received by a local newspaper, the Wichita Eagle, and contained a letter from a person who claimed to have murdered Vicki Wegerle in 1986. Enclosed were numerous photographs of the crime scene and a copy of the victim's driver's license. At this point, Wegerle was not a confirmed victim of BTK. Under her finger nails, police found essential and previously unknown evidence. Armed with this data, they began to test over a thousand men.

While this was happening, Rader continued to send letters and packages. One contained chapter titles for something called the "BTK Story." Another was a package discovered attached to a signpost in Wichita. Inside were graphic recollections of the first family Rader murdered and a lurid sketch. Further chapter titles were found, one named "A Serial Killer Is Born." In the next package, BTK confessed to the murder of Jake Allen, a nineteen-year-old from Argonia in Kansas. This murder was recent and had only been committed a month previous. In spite of the claims, the death was later ruled a suicide. In October, a package was sent containing images of terrorized children, with an accompanying poem that threatened the case's lead investigator. There were still further details of the "BTK Story," including autobiographical accounts of some of the murders.

Another package contained the driver's license of a known victim of BTK, Nancy Fox. There was also a doll that had been bound at the hands and feet. Rader had even tied a plastic bag over the doll's head. Not all the messages got through successfully. One was left in the back of a truck but disposed of by the driver. In a later communication, Rader sent the authorities searching for it as he questioned what had become of the box. When reviewing security footage from the car park where Rader had originally placed the package, investigators could make out a shadowy figure driving a Jeep. Taking the model and specifications of the car, they began to search. More packages were sent, often containing further details of BTK's murders and more bound-up dolls. One was designed to replicate the murder of Josephine Otero, the eleven-year-old who had been part of the first family murdered by Rader.

Perhaps the most important clue came after Rader asked them a direct question in a letter. He quizzed them as to whether it would be safe to send them some of his digital documents stored on a floppy disk. Answering via the newspaper, the police informed Rader that it would be perfectly fine for him to send such documents and that they would be unable to trace him. Rader complied and sent a new package. Inside was a stolen gold necklace and a photocopied front cover of a book about serial killers. At the bottom of the box was a floppy disk. Opening the item, the police scanned it for information. After a cursory sweep, nothing useful was found. But by digging deeper and retrieving the lost metadata on the disk, investigators were able to uncover bits of information. There was a document that had been deleted from the disk but was able to be recovered. The information inside pointed towards the Christ Lutheran Church. The last person who had modified the document was a person named Dennis. An internet search pointed them to one Dennis Rader, the president of a church council who shared the name. In a drive-by of his house, they noticed a black Jeep parked in the driveway.

After years of having no case against BTK, it seemed that the killer's letters were leading the authorities straight to his home. With the evidence in hand, they got a warrant to test a DNA sample left by Rader's daughter at a local university. It matched the sample taken from Vicki Wegerle. Finally, there was enough information and evidence available for an arrest.

Dennis Rader was arrested while driving on the February 25th, 2005. During the arrest, one officer asked Rader whether he knew why he might be being arrested. He replied that he had his suspicions. At the same time as the arrest, police officials fell upon Rader's home and a combination of local police, FBI agents, and ATF agents searched through the house and

Rader's vehicles. They also searched through his church and the library where he accessed the Internet. At a press conference the next day, the authorities happily announced that BTK had been arrested.

In all, Dennis Rader was charged with ten murders over the course of many years. His bail was set at $10 million while Rader watched on via video link. Not speaking at his arraignment, his public defender entered a plea of not guilty. Before the trial started, this was changed to a guilty plea. During the trial, Rader was able to describe each murder in detail and showed no remorse.

This would change at the sentencing. After the families were allowed to make statements, Rader proceeded to ramble for thirty minutes, apologizing for his crimes and continuing his speech in a manner likened by one attorney to the acceptance of an academy award. He was handed ten consecutive life sentences. He would not be eligible for parole for one hundred and seventy five years. He is set to serve the majority of his time in solitary confinement, for his own protection.

As well as the cold case of the ten murders of the BTK killer, many agencies poured over their own case files to see whether they could link Rader's actions to any unsolved crimes. In spite of a lengthy review, the only cold cases solved by his arrest were those originally attributed to him. In terms of cold cases, Dennis Rader is perhaps the only serial killer to have trapped himself after seeming to get away.

16th Street Baptist Church

Where: Birmingham, Alabama
When: September 15, 1963
Suspect(s): Members of the United Klans of America
Conviction: November 18, 1977 and other dates.

Background Information

Over the course of this book, we have examined many different varieties of cold cases. Mostly, they have reached a dead end as a result of a lack of evidence. But this is not the only reason why a case might go cold. When considering the example of the bombing of the 16th Street Baptist Church in Birmingham, Alabama, there are additional reasons why the case might not have been pursued in the most rigorous fashion.

Dr. Martin Luther King had described Birmingham as probably the most segregated place in America, extending a long-standing reputation as a hotbed of racial tensions. Public facilities such as schools, buses, and drinking fountains were segregated. Any attempt to reform this segregation was met with outrage and often a violent resistance. During this time, bombings at historically African-American properties and churches became increasingly common. In the years preceding the event in question, twenty-one separate bombings had taken place. Luckily, no one had been killed, but the explosions were enough to lead many to nickname the city 'Bombingham.'

One of the key centers of the African-American community was the 16th Street Baptist Church. It was used as a gathering point for civil rights activists. Dr. Martin Luther King, Fred Shuttlesworth, and Ralph David Abernathy all held meetings there. During the months leading up to the bombing, it had been the center point for voter registration and desegregation activities. Public schools had recently been integrated. This had been met with fierce opposition. Among those expressing frustration was the local members of the Ku Klux Klan.

The Day of the Tragedy

On the day of the bombing, Thomas Edwin Blanton Jr., Robert Edward Chambliss, Herman Frank Cash, and Bobby Frank Cherry all arrived at the church. They were members of the United Klans of America. Moving around the grounds, they laid fifteen stick of dynamite. All were fitted with a delayed action timer and were placed under the steps of the church, near the basement.

At just after twenty past ten in the morning, the church received an anonymous phone call. A fourteen-year-old named Carolyn Maull answered the phone. An unidentified voice simply said the words, "three minutes," and hung up. Less than a minute later, the dynamite exploded. At the moment of the blast, five children were in the basement preparing for church. The explosion rattled the building and threw occupants across the room.

A hole seven feet wide was blown in the rear wall of the church. It left a five-foot crater in the church. The explosion was large enough to knock a passing motorist from his car. Nearby windows were shattered. The only stained glass window left in the church depicted Jesus leading a young group of children in prayer.

Hundreds of people ran to the church to search for the injured. Despite sustaining wounds themselves, people searched through the debris. It is thought that over two thousand African-Americans arrived on the scene. They were outraged. The local pastor tried to calm the mood. One witness recalled seeing just one white person in attendance, Robert Chambliss, a known member of the Klan. He stood motionless, observing in a detached manner.

Four girls were killed in the attack, their ages ranging from eleven to fourteen. They had not only been killed by the blast, but had also in some cases been mutilated. One girl was only identifiable by her ring. A further twenty people were severely injured in the explosion, one of whom was a girl who was hit in the face with more than twenty shards of glass. She lost the sight in one eye.

Despite the death toll and the damage caused by the bombs, the case remained unsolved. It was deemed a cold case, with investigators not able or not willing to chase down the leads that existed following the bombing of the church. This would remain the case for eight years, until William Baxley was elected as the Attorney General of Alabama. Within a week of being in office, Baxley had launched an investigation into the blast.

The Investigation

During his investigation, Baxley examined the old case files available to him. On looking through the files, he discovered that many of the investigations were inefficient and lackluster, with leads not pursued to the proper end points. The case was formally reopened in 1971. At this time, Baxley worked to build trust with the key witnesses. He was eventually able to identify Chambliss as being at the scene. Not only this, but he was also able to gain information that told of how Chambliss had purchased the dynamite from a local store in the two weeks leading up to the bombing. Using this information and other witness accounts, he began to build the case against Chambliss.

He requested to be allowed to review the FBI's files on the incident. Here, he discovered that the evidence collected by the Bureau had not been shared with the local authorities. It took Baxley until 1976 to be allowed to use the full range of materials the FBI had in its possession. It was only when he threatened to go public that the FBI acquiesced to his request.

The Trial

The trial of Robert Chambliss began on the 14th of November, 1977. At this time, Chambliss was seventy-three years old. Despite being originally charged with four counts of murder, the judge ruled that Chambliss would only stand trial for one, the death of Carol Denise McNair. During the trial, Chambliss was able to remain a free man, thanks to the two hundred thousand dollar bail he had paid. The amount had been raised by family members and those who supported him. He pleaded not guilty.

Chambliss insisted that although he had purchased the dynamite, he had given it to fellow Klan member Gary Thomas Rowe, Jr.

Baxley set about discrediting Chambliss version of events, pointing the finger clearly at Chambliss as the bomber. One of the most important members of the prosecution was Chambliss's own niece, Reverend Elizabeth Cobbs. She informed the court that her uncle had repeatedly told her of his "one man battle" against the African-American community since the 1940s. He had also told Rev. Cobbs on the morning of the bomb blast that he possessed enough dynamite to destroy half of Birmingham. When reading a newspaper about the bombing a week later, Chambliss had commented to his niece that the bomb had never been designed to kill anyone but instead went off too early. Also interviewed were witnesses who had been in the Ku Klux Klan at the same time as Chambliss and remembered his regret that the group was not active enough in discouraging racial integration.

In closing, Baxley admitted to the judge that Chambliss was not the only bomber. He commented that Carol Denise McNair's birthday would have been the very next day, had she lived. He appealed to the jury to return a guilty verdict. The jury deliberated matters for six hours and continued into the next day. When they returned, they delivered a verdict of guilty. Chambliss was sentenced to life in prison. Even after the verdict, Chambliss protested his innocence.

But Baxley was not finished. Knowing the names of those he believed to also be involved, he immediately issued a subpoena to Thomas Blanton, demanding his presence in court. Though he lacked the right evidence to convict Blanton, Baxley hoped to panic the man into revealing his co-conspirators in exchange for a softer sentence. It did not work. Later, Chambliss would attempt to appeal his conviction but had his appeal turned down. He would die aged eighty-one in 1985, still in custody. During his time in prison, Chambliss had continued to protest his innocence and pointed the finger at Gary Thomas Rowe Jr. as the real mastermind behind the bombing.

Continuing the Investigation and the Trial

A decade after Chambliss died, the FBI reopened the investigation into the church bombing. With this reopening of a case that had again seemed to go cold, they also unsealed over nine thousand pieces of evidence. They announced their findings publically, suggesting that the bombing had been committed by Ku Klux Klan members. Four Klan members had formed a splinter group named the Cahaba Boys. They were the ones who carried out the bombing. As well as Chambliss, the group included Thomas Edwin Blanton Jr., Herman Frank Cash, and Bobby Frank Cherry. Chambliss and Cash had both passed away at this point, but arrest warrants were issued for the remaining two.

Both men were indicted by a grand jury and surrendered themselves to the police. Among the evidence used during the trial were audio recordings taken by the FBI in which Blanton discussed planning to plant a bomb with other Klan members during an argument with his wife. As well as this, Cherry's ex-wife spoke about her former husband's confession that he had been the one to plant the bomb. He had mentioned regret that children had died but seemed buoyed by the fact that they would not be able to reproduce. Both men were convicted of four counts of first degree murder for their role in the bombing of the church.

Looking back at the trials, Baxley commented that he regretted not being allowed to access the audio recordings during his own time in office. Had he been able to use these tapes as evidence, he might have been able to pursue the men of his own volition. But in saying this, he did confess that the racial tension in 1960s Birmingham would have hindered the court's abilities to host a fair trial.

As a side note, it is interesting to note that the FBI case was originally blocked in 1963 by J. Edgar Hoover himself, the head of the FBI. Not only did he block the prosecution at this time, but he officially closed the case in 1968.

The Aftermath

With tensions remaining high in the years following the bombing of the church in Alabama, it took many decades for the men involved to finally see punishment for their crimes. At this point, four men have been convicted of the bombing of 16th Street Baptist Church. Despite the mass of evidence that existed (and was later enough to reach a conviction), the case was deemed cold, not by the lack of evidence, but by the circumstances surrounding the pursuit of civil rights during the time period. As such, it is important to note that cold cases are not always simply cases that have reached their natural end. Sometimes, they are ended far too soon.

Conclusion

When investigating a crime, the evidence that is immediately available can be difficult to discern. Interpreting this information is a key part of any investigation. Being able to accurately put together all of the clues and come to the conclusion of who the perpetrator is can be incredibly difficult. Despite the skills of some detectives, there are still a number of cases that simply go cold. The crime might have been elegantly planned, the evidence might have been destroyed, or the conditions for a successful prosecution simply might not exist. There are many reasons why it might not be possible to solve a criminal investigation.

However, as we have seen in this book, that does not mean the end of the road. As we look back over the cases that were never solved, we must now ask ourselves which cases might be able to be solved in the near future. Just as DNA was a key factor in many of the cases we have examined, what will be the next step forward that allows us to finally reach a conclusion on some of these unsolved cases?

Bonus Chapter from Andrew J. Clark's book Vanished Chilling True Stories of Missing Persons

Just Click on the cover to check it out.

The criminal mastermind who vanished when jumping from a plane

Who: D.B. Cooper

When: November 24, 1971

Where: The airspace between Portland and Seattle

Context

Perhaps the most famous case of a missing person in American history, the story of D. B. (or Dan) Cooper involves a criminal heist, a fantastic getaway, and an enduring mythology. For those who have dreamed of a big score or the perfect crime, the disappearance of Cooper is the story to aspire to.

On that day

It goes like this. On the day before Thanksgiving in 1971, a man naming himself Dan Cooper got onto Flight 305 on Northwest Airlines, which was going to fly from Portland to Seattle. Descriptions given at the time put him in a dark-colored suit with a black tie, witnesses suggesting that he looked like an executive or a business man of some type. During the flight, Cooper gestured towards his briefcase, revealing to the stewardess the bomb which he had smuggled aboard. Using the bomb, he hijacked the plane. The plane was forced to land, arriving in Seattle where the hijacker demanded $200,000 in cash, four parachutes, and enough food to supply himself and the crew. The passengers were turned free, while the flight took to the air with Cooper, the money, a flight attendant, and three pilots still aboard. The bills had been marked, meaning Cooper would be caught should he want to spend any of his illicit gains. They headed south. It was dark and there was a light rain. After forty-five minutes, he sent the stewardess to check the cockpit while he began ready the parachute. He tied the bag containing the money to his body, lowered the rear set of stairs and just above the dark forests of wintery Portland, he jumped out. When the flight landed, all that was found was two remaining parachutes, an empty seat, and a black tie.

The investigation

As soon as the hijacked plane left the airport, authorities scrambled planes and helicopters to track the plane. They missed Cooper's exit from the plane, trailing the hijacked jet to Seattle. Over the next days, the military ordered a thousand men to sweep the area where Cooper was thought to have landed. One method of investigation involved flying the original plane over the ocean and throwing man-shaped objects from the plane door. Using this method, the investigators hoped to learn about the trajectory Cooper had taken on exiting the plane and to clarify their search in the forest, but it came to no avail. Even the top-secret SR-71 Blackbird spy plane was used to photograph the forest to try and find any trace of the man. They found nothing.

The investigation continued for many years. In 1980, just north of the Columbia River, three bundles of cash were discovered by Brian Ingram, a boy who was creating a pit for a fire in a location known as Tena Bar. Hidden just inches below the snow, the bundles still had their elastic bands attached. With the serial numbers matching $5,800 of Cooper's marked notes, the FBI began to sweep the area. They analyzed river beds and dredged the water. Again, nothing was found.

Even as recently as 2007, the FBI was willing to trust the case to Special Agent Larry Carr, providing he was able to keep costs and time to a minimum. Carr's method of detection approached the hijacking as he might approach a bank robbery, interviewing and discussing the case with as many members of the public as possible. Though he was able to unearth several new pieces of information, there was still no trace of the man or the remainder of the money.

Update

For many Americans, the case of Dan Cooper has now passed into legend. The missing man and his money are treated in a manner similar to the bank robbers of the old west, their fame enduring. Because of this, the discussion of his crime is now a hobby and a notable interest for many people. For these individuals, the case rests on a few salient questions.

The first is whether Cooper died when jumping from the plane. Because no body was ever discovered and no person ever surfaced with the money, it has been hard to pronounce the suspect dead. When considering the jump, skydivers of varying experience levels have claimed that he faced a difficult prospect. For the first-time jumper, a sure death awaited. For the experienced sky diver, however, safety could be reached. Once out of the plane and landed, the cold weather could have affected his survival chances, but again, no body was discovered. For those debating the question of Cooper's experience levels, the request for both front and back parachutes points to an amateur jumper, while the fact that he refused attempts to instruct him how to jump indicate that he was assured enough in his own abilities. That he chose to use the parachute which he could not steer suggests a lowered chance of survival and a lack of experience, but the stewardess's description of him assuredly putting on the parachute seems to point to a well-practiced man.

For some, the finding of the money by Brian Ingram adds complexion to the story. Twenty miles away from the money's resting spot is the town of Ariel, the very place an analysis of the drop zone suggested Cooper would end up. For some, this suggests that the money had washed along a smaller series of rivers to rest at Tena Bar. Another theory posits that Cooper actually landed at Tena Bar and needed to bury his money to avert the chase of the FBI. Even more outlandish is the prospect of a person burying a small amount of marked bills to throw the authorities off the correct scent.

One investigation is known as the Palmer Report and was commissioned by the FBI to provide an analysis of the sand bar where the money was found. During the time between the incident and the finding of the money, the Columbia River was dredged, and different sand was moved on to the Tena Var. The Palmer Report found that the money was found in a top layer of the sand which had been deposited before the dredging. Because of this, it can be assumed that the money was elsewhere before it finally came to rest in this place. Those who reject this theory point to the fact that the rubber bands remained in place despite their delicacy.

The path of the flight has even been questioned. The original path map which is found in the archive of the FBI has no information about how or when it was created. As drawn, this map is supposedly from a close analysis of the flight recordings and the data from radar stations. This detailed path flies in a direction which does not include Tena Bar or anywhere near the suspected areas. Because of this, confusion over the possible washing away of the money becomes even more difficult to discern and quantify. Figuring out how Cooper's money washed down the river using the FBI flight path is difficult. The question of how three separate bundles of marked bills managed to separate from the rest of the ransom is also hard to answer. It might be that the bank's provided bag protected the money for years until disintegrating, or that Cooper lost the money during his jump or his landing. It could even be that they were buried by someone at a later date as a deliberate misdirection.

Unlike other missing person cases, one of the most intriguing factors in the case of Dan Cooper is that we don't know his prior identity. He might have been from the area, allowing him to recognize it from above. Even the fact that he is quoted as asking for "negotiable American currency" suggests someone who might not even have been local to America. After all these years, finding D. B. Cooper is still one of the most infamous cases of a missing person. It is a case that may never be solved.

Further Reading

Aron, P. (1998). *Unsolved mysteries of American history*. New York: Wiley.

Branson, J. and Branson, M. (2011). *Delayed justice*. Amherst, N.Y.: Prometheus Books.

Douglas, J. and Olshaker, M. (2001). *The cases that haunt us*. New York: Pocket Books.

Halber, D. (n.d.). *The skeleton crew*.

Newton, M. (2009). *The encyclopedia of unsolved crimes*. New York: Facts on File.

Odell, R. (2010). *The mammoth book of bizarre crimes*. Philadelphia, Pa.: Running Press Book Pub.

Philbin, T. (2012). *The killer book of cold cases*. Naperville, Ill.: Sourcebooks.

Ramsland, K. (2004). *The science of Cold case files*. New York: Berkley Boulevard Books.

Printed in Germany
by Amazon Distribution
GmbH, Leipzig